Creative Creations

for your Cat

EASY DO-IT-YOURSELF PROJECTS TO MAKE FOR YOUR FAVORITE PET

Norma Martinez
Carlota Cirera

Skyhorse Publishing

Contents

All cats behave differently and some may destroy these toys more than others, so we recommend that you always KEEP AN EYE ON YOUR CAT while he or she is playing, because there is a risk that the cat may break or eat part of the toy. You should also CHECK THE TOYS when the cat is done playing to make sure there are no parts that are worn out that should be changed.

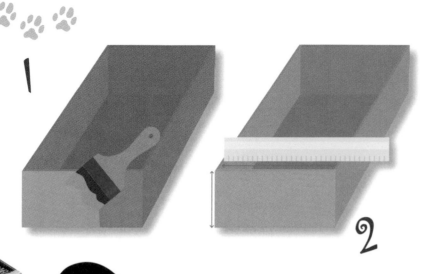

1. To make this scratching box, you will need a short cardboard box. You could also cut a shoe box to the right size. Paint the box any color you like.

2. Measure the inside of the box like you see in the drawing. You need to know its length and height.

Scratching Box

3. Now you need some pieces of corrugated cardboard, the ones with a wavy section in the middle. Draw rectangles with a pencil that are the length and height of the box you just measured. Make sure the corrugated wavy side of the cardboard is on the long side of the rectangle.

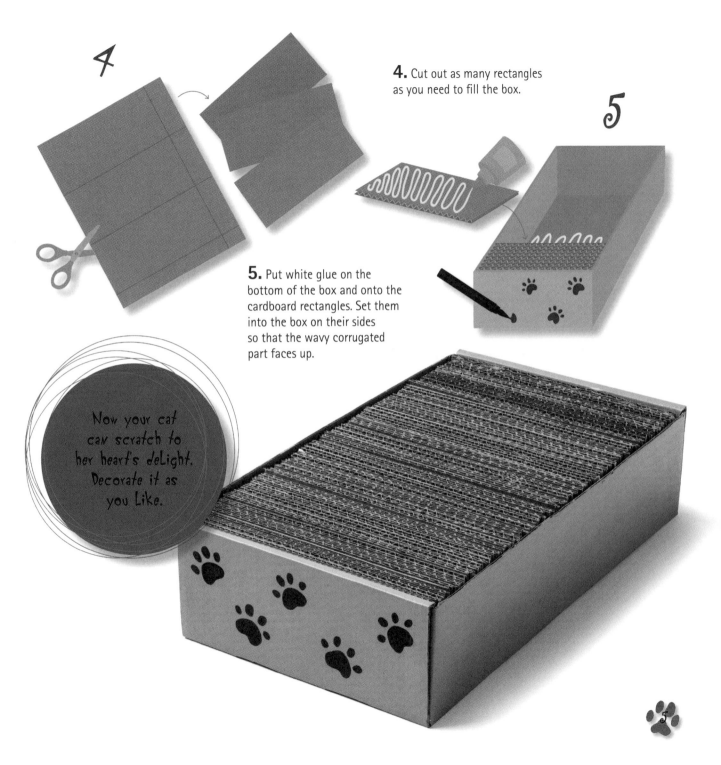

4. Cut out as many rectangles as you need to fill the box.

5. Put white glue on the bottom of the box and onto the cardboard rectangles. Set them into the box on their sides so that the wavy corrugated part faces up.

Now your cat can scratch to her heart's delight. Decorate it as you like.

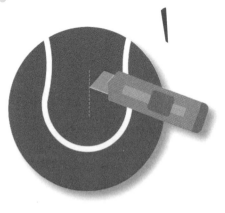

1. Cut into a tennis ball.

2. Put two bells inside the ball so that the toy makes noise when it moves.

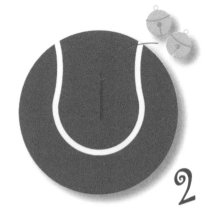

Tennis Ball

3

3. Cut a rectangle out of the fabric you want to wrap the ball in several times (you can use an old t-shirt). Cut fringes into the sides that don't reach the ball as shown in the drawing.

4. Wrap the ball in the fabric.

5. Tie the sides of the fabric so that the ball doesn't come out. It will end up looking like a piece of candy. Keep an eye on your cat when she is playing to make sure she doesn't hurt herself, and check the toy when your cat is done playing.

If your cat has ripped out a lot of the fringes, you can wrap the ball in stronger fabric.

1. To make this dispenser toy, you need the inside of a roll of paper towels and wrapping paper with a pretty design. Trace the circle of the end of the tube onto the back of the wrapping paper, so you can't see the pencil marks. Do this twice and then cut out the two circles, leaving extra space around them.

2. Cut tabs into the paper circles without going over the pencil marks.

Dispenser Tube

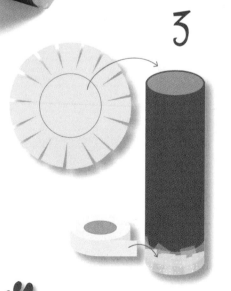

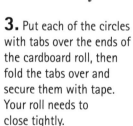

3. Put each of the circles with tabs over the ends of the cardboard roll, then fold the tabs over and secure them with tape. Your roll needs to close tightly.

4. Roll the tube in more wrapping paper. Use tape or washi tape to stick it to the tube.

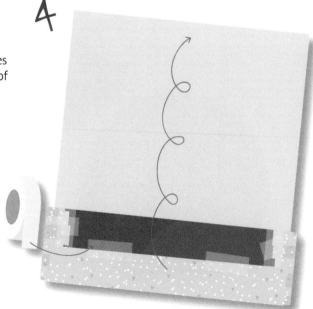

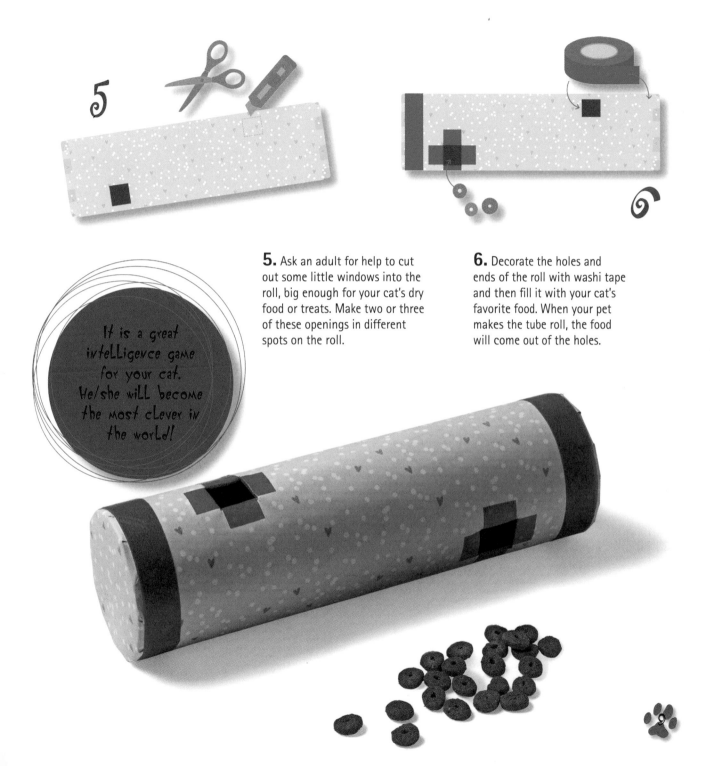

5. Ask an adult for help to cut out some little windows into the roll, big enough for your cat's dry food or treats. Make two or three of these openings in different spots on the roll.

6. Decorate the holes and ends of the roll with washi tape and then fill it with your cat's favorite food. When your pet makes the tube roll, the food will come out of the holes.

It is a great intelligence game for your cat. He/she will become the most clever in the world!

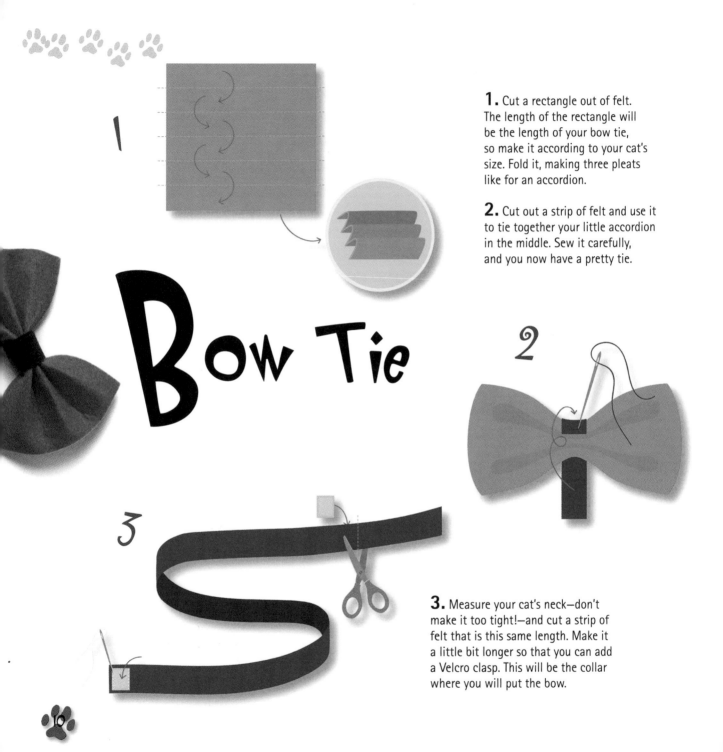

1. Cut a rectangle out of felt. The length of the rectangle will be the length of your bow tie, so make it according to your cat's size. Fold it, making three pleats like for an accordion.

2. Cut out a strip of felt and use it to tie together your little accordion in the middle. Sew it carefully, and you now have a pretty tie.

Bow Tie

3. Measure your cat's neck—don't make it too tight!—and cut a strip of felt that is this same length. Make it a little bit longer so that you can add a Velcro clasp. This will be the collar where you will put the bow.

4. Sew one piece of Velcro on the back of the bow tie and the other in the middle of the collar.

5. Make more colored bow ties, and then you can change them when you like.

When your cat grows up, you will probably have to make new bow ties for her or him.

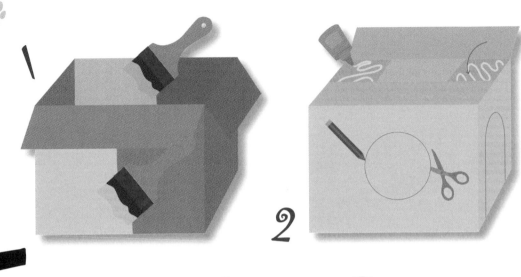

Funny Face Box

1. Find a cardboard box that is big enough for your cat to fit inside. Close the bottom flaps of the box with glue or packing tape, paint the outside and inside, and let it dry.

2. Close the top flaps with white glue. Draw and cut out circles on three sides of the box, which have to be big enough for your cat's head to fit through. On the fourth side, make a little cat door.

3. Trace or photocopy the patterns on page 35 to decorate one of the holes in the box like it were a lion's head. You can make the size of the pattern bigger or smaller, depending on the box you are using. Trace the pattern onto felt and cut out the shapes.

12

4. Put white glue onto the lion's mane and put it over the hole on one side of the box. Make sure the felt mane is lined up over the hole in the box.

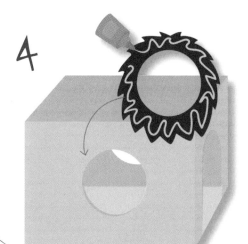

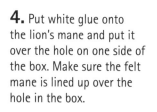

You can also put some decorations on the door of the box.

5. Do the same with the lion's ears. Now, when your cat sticks its head out the hole, it will look like a lion! Decorate the other two holes with other animals or designs like —for example—a shark or a flower.

1. Photocopy and cut out the patterns on page 34. Trace the outlines onto felt with a pencil and cut them out. Use different colors for the body and the ears.

1

Mice CoupLe

2

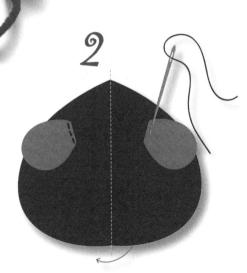

2. Carefully sew the mouse's ears onto the body as shown in the drawing. Then fold the body in half, making sure the ears are on the outside.

3. Sew the mouse's body, but leave an opening through which you can put the stuffing. Sew slowly and carefully.

3

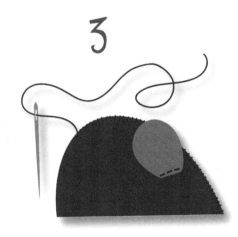

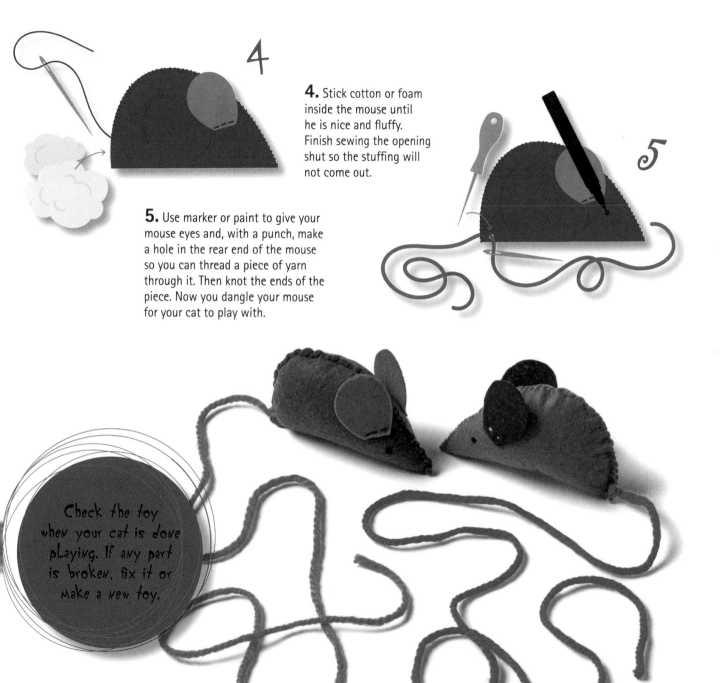

4. Stick cotton or foam inside the mouse until he is nice and fluffy. Finish sewing the opening shut so the stuffing will not come out.

5. Use marker or paint to give your mouse eyes and, with a punch, make a hole in the rear end of the mouse so you can thread a piece of yarn through it. Then knot the ends of the piece. Now you dangle your mouse for your cat to play with.

Check the toy when your cat is done playing. If any part is broken, fix it or make a new toy.

1. To make this scoop for the cat litter, you need a bottle with a handle, like those for fabric softener or detergent. The larger the bottle is, the bigger the scoop will be. Cut off the top of the handle as shown in the drawing. If it is hard for you to use scissors, ask an adult to help you with a box cutter.

Bottle Scoop

2

2. Cut the bottom of your scoop to round the edges and retouch the sides to make it into your favorite shape.

3. Decorate the handle of the scoop by wrapping it with colored tape.

3

5

4

4. Carefully make a small hole at the top of the handle with a punch.

5. String a piece of rope through the hole and knot it. Hang the scoop wherever you like and use it to clean the cat litter.

You could make another one for your cat's dry food too.

FLuffy SNake

1. Take an old pair of tights and cut off one leg, like you see in the drawing.

2. Stuff it with cotton, stuffing from an old cushion, foam, etc.

2

3. Keep tying small sections off with small pieces of rope to create your snake's body, adding more stuffing if your snake is too skinny. Put two bells inside the last section, so that it makes noise when your cat plays with it.

3

4. Make a knot at the end so the stuffing and bells do not fall out, and then cut off any excess.

4

5

5. Cut two small circles out of white felt and draw pupils in the middle. Sew them onto the snake's heads to make its eyes.

Keep an eye on your cat while he/she is playing to make sure he/she doesn't hurt himself.

19

1. To make your treat container, you need a glass jar. You probably have one around the house. Photocopy the pattern on page 34, cut it out and copy the outline onto your jar.

Treat Jar

3. Use the pattern on page 34 to make the tag for the jar. Trace the outline in pencil onto poster board and cut it out.

2

2. Paint the outline with chalkboard paint.

3

4. Make a hole in the tag using a hole punch and then decorate it. You could also write your cat's name on the tag.

5. Wrap a piece of string around the top of the jar, then string the cat tag through it and make a bow. On the outline in chalkboard paint, draw any picture you want, or write the expiration date of the food you fill the jar with, or even draw a picture of your cat. Use the jar for your cat's favorite treat.

Try to make the tag with colored cardboard, or even felt. Have fun creating!

CHLOE

1. To make this tassel, cut a square out of cardboard and wrap yarn around it. Wrap it many times so you will get a nice fat tassel. The length of the cardboard will be how long your yarn tassel is.

Yarn Tassels

2. When you have finished, thread a piece of yarn under all the pieces you just wrapped.

3. Make a strong knot to hold the yarn in place.

4. Put scissors between the yarn and cardboard and cut all the pieces. Your tassel is almost ready!

5. Gather all the fringes of the tassel together and wrap another color of yarn around the top as shown in the drawing. Now you can hang your tassel from a doorknob or from wherever you like. Keep an eye on your cat while he/she is playing to make sure he doesn't hurt himself.

4

5

If you place the tassels in a place where the air runs, they will move and catch the attention of your cat.

1. Paint a shoebox your favorite color.

2. Make several holes in the sides and lid of the box. You can use the pattern on page 34 if you like. Remember that the holes have to be big enough for your cat's paw to fit through, so don't make them too small.

3. To make sure your cat can't open the box, glue on the top with white glue.

InteLLigence Game

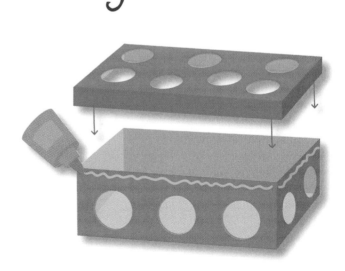

4. You can use clothespins to fasten the lid onto the box while the glue dries. When the glue is nice and dry, remove the clothespins and decorate the box with a marker.

5. Put your cat's favorite treats and games inside the box. It will have to figure out how to get the objects out by sticking its paw through the holes.

This game is perfect for sharpening your furry friend's intelligence.

1. To make this cat cushion, you will need a large t-shirt. The larger the t-shirt is, the bigger your cushion will be. Stretch the t-shirt out over a table and cut out the front and back together in a rectangular or square shape.

Knotted Cushion

2. With the two pieces of fabric completely aligned, cut out the four corners as shown in the drawing.

3. Cut fringes into every side, which you will later tie into knots. Don't make them too narrow, because then they may rip when you knot them.

4

5

4. Take the two fringes that are on top and bottom and knot them. Keep on making knots, but leave several so that you have room to put the stuffing in.

5. Fill the cushion so it is nice and soft, and then finishing knotting all the fringes so that no filling can come out.
Your cushion is ready!

Remind your parents
or older siblings
that you can transform
shirts that they
no longer use!

1. To make this fish-on-a-line toy, trace or photocopy the pattern on page 34, cut it out and trace the outline onto different colors of felt. Make two pieces in each color.

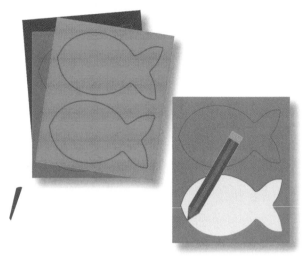

1

String of Fish

2

2. Cut them out.

3. Make a hole in the middle of all your felt fish with a punch, so that you can string yarn through them.

3

4. Cut a piece of yarn as long as you want your toy to be, and then tie a bell onto one end. Make several knots so it doesn't slip off.

5. Using a yarn needle, thread one fish and then one pompom onto your yarn, alternating them. After you have all the pompoms and fish on the yarn, knot the end so they don't fall off and . . . you're ready to play with your cat!

Check the toy when your cat is done to make sure that it is still in good conditions.

Photo Frame

1. To make this picture frame, you just need the lid of a shoebox. Line the sides with crepe paper. Tip: If you put use layers of crepe paper, it will look better.

2. Measure the inside of the box.

3. Pick a piece of wrapping paper that you really like, cut it out to the measurements of the inside of the lid and glue it on.

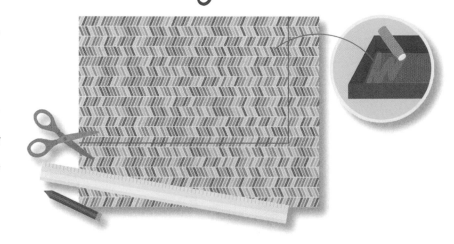

This can be a good gift for someone who has a pet. Like you.

4. Make two small holes using a punch or other sharp object on the two sides of the lid. Do this carefully so that the holes are at the same height. Ask someone for help if you need it. Put a piece of string through the holes.

5. Tie several knots at each end so the rope doesn't come out, and now you can hang your frame. Fasten on photos of your cat with small clips.

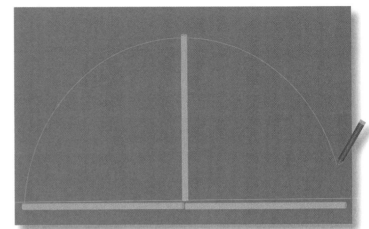

1. To make this toy, you will need five sticks long enough for the tent (so that your cat can fit inside). Pick a piece of fabric you like. Lay three of the sticks on the fabric, like you see in the image, and draw a semicircle, using the sticks as a guide.

Easy Tent

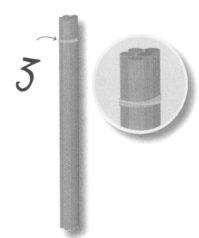

2. Cut the fabric out; you will use it to cover your tent.

3. Put the five sticks together and fasten them with a rubber band.

4. Open the sticks up to create the tent, and then tie it all together again with a piece of string, so that they remain separated. Tie it well with the rope and remember to wrap the rope under and over all the sticks.

A perfect tent so your cat can rest peacefully!

5. Take the straight part of the fabric and lay it over the stick structure, with the round part at the bottom. Using the same piece of rope, tie the fabric around the top so it doesn't fall off. You can use white glue to fasten the fabric to the sticks.

Patterns

MICE COUPLE
PAGE 14

TREAT JAR
PAGE 20

TREAT JAR
PAGE 20
and
STRING OF FISH
PAGE 28

INTELLIGENCE GAME
PAGE 24

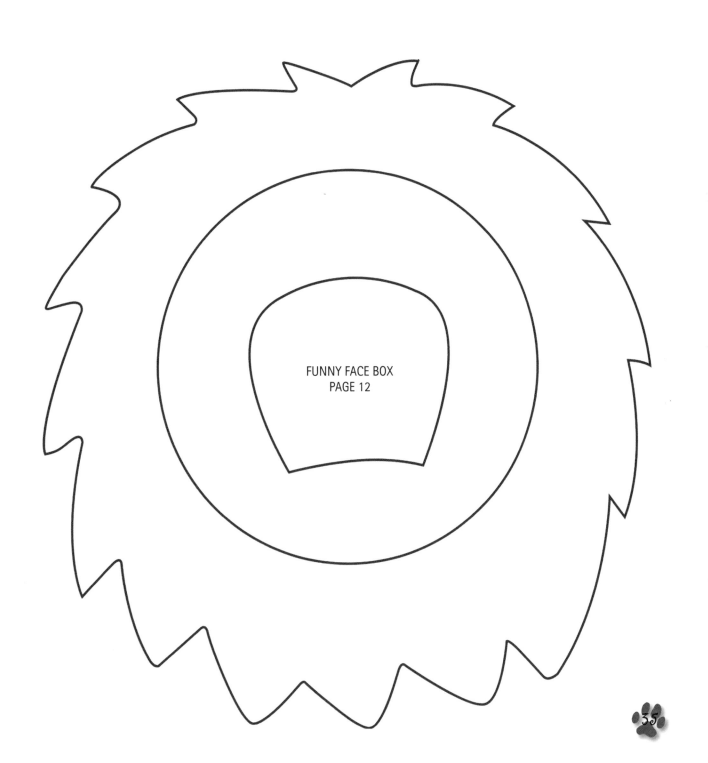

FUNNY FACE BOX
PAGE 12

35

Skyhorse Publishing books may be purchased in bulk at special discounts for sales promotion, corporate gifts, fund-raising, or educational purposes. Special editions can also be created to specifications. For details, contact the Special Sales Department, Skyhorse Publishing, 307 West 36th Street, 11th Floor, New York, NY 10018 or info@skyhorsepublishing.com.

For details, contact the Special Sales Department, Skyhorse Publishing, 307 West 36th Street, 11th Floor, New York, NY 10018 or info@skyhorsepublishing.com.

Skyhorse® and Skyhorse Publishing® are registered trademarks of Skyhorse Publishing, Inc.®, a Delaware corporation.

Visit our website at www.skyhorsepublishing.com.

10 9 8 7 6 5 4 3 2 1

Library of Congress Cataloging-in-Publication Data is available on file.

Projects and illustrations: Norma Martínez and Carlota Cirera

Design and layout: Estudi Guasch, S.L.

Photography (cats): stock.adobe.com and AGE Fotostock

Photography (crafts): Pep Herrero

Cover design by Michael Short

Print ISBN: 978-1-63158-315-5
E-Book ISBN: 978-1-63158-319-3

Printed in Canada